A Kid's Guide to INCREDIBLE TECHNOLOGY™

The Incredible Story of Telescopes

Greg Roza

The Rosen Publishing Group's
PowerKids Press™
New York

For Autumn

Published in 2004 by The Rosen Publishing Group, Inc.
29 East 21st Street, New York, NY 10010

First Edition

Editor: Kathy Kuhtz Campbell
Book Design: Mike Donnellan

Illustration Credits: Alessandro Bartolozzi, Leonello Calvetti, Lorenzo Cecchi.
Photo Credits: p. 4 © Reuters NewMedia Inc./CORBIS; pp. 4 (inset), 11, 12, 16, 19 © Roger Ressmeyer/CORBIS; p. 7 © Jose Fuste Raga/CORBIS.

Roza, Greg.
The incredible story of telescopes / Greg Roza.— 1st ed.
    v. cm.— (A kid's guide to incredible technology)
Includes bibliographical references and index.
Contents: The invention of the telescope—How light works—Lenses and mirrors—How a refraction telescope works—How a reflection telescope works—Making a primary mirror—Housing a large telescope: observatories—The Hubble telescope—How the Hubble telescope looks into space—The future of telescope technology.
  ISBN 0-8239-6715-8 (lib. bdg.)
1. Telescopes—Juvenile literature. [1. Telescopes.] I. Title. II. Series.
  QB88 .R79 2004
  681'.4123—dc21

                                                                                    2002152076

Manufactured in the United States of America

Contents

What Are Telescopes?

Telescopes are instruments that make faraway objects seem larger and closer than they really are. **Astronomers** use telescopes to study planets, stars, **galaxies**, and other objects in the heavens. The objects are so far away from us that it takes their light billions of years to reach us. When we look through the eyepiece of a telescope, we are seeing images of some distant objects as they appeared billions of years ago, not as they look today.

There are many kinds of telescopes. There are **optical** telescopes, such as the 33-foot-wide (10-m-wide) twin Keck telescopes in Hawaii. There are also **radio** telescopes, such as the 1,000-foot-wide (304.8-m-wide) Arecibo radio telescope in Puerto Rico. Telescopes can even orbit, or move in a circular path, around Earth, as does **NASA**'s Hubble Space Telescope.

In April 2001, the Hubble Space Telescope took this picture of star patterns in the Whirlpool galaxy. Inset: Keck II, a giant telescope, enables astronomers to explore deep space. The more light a telescope collects, the fainter the object it can see.

How Light Works

Optical telescope **technology** is based on the science of how light works. Light is a kind of energy called **radiation**. There are many forms of radiation, including radio waves and **X rays**, but light is the only kind we can see. Our eyes see images when light rays **reflect**, or bounce, off an object and meet at a single point inside each eye. Just as our eyes do, telescopes collect and **focus** light at a single point to create an image of faraway objects. Most optical telescopes use lenses or mirrors to form images of objects. Telescopes can focus light by reflecting light from a surface, such as a mirror. They can also refract, or bend, light by slowing it down. Passing light through a glass lens refracts it. The bigger the telescope lens or mirror, the more light that telescope can collect and focus. The resulting image can then be viewed through an eyepiece or be collected to make pictures on film.

Left: *An image of the U.S. Capitol is reflected in a pool on the Mall in Washington, D.C. Mirrors in telescopes are used to reflect light waves in a similar way to that of a pool of water.* Right: *As light passes through space, it is bent, similar to the way a pencil appears to be bent when placed into a glass of water. This is refraction.*

TECH KNOWLEDGE

The science of light is called optics. Light travels at about 186,000 miles per second (299,338 km/s). In just 1 second, light can travel around Earth eight times!

Eyepiece

Wooden Tube

Primary Lens

Secondary Mirror

Eyepiece

Telescope Mounting

Primary Mirror

Telescope Beginnings

Most historians believe that a Dutch eyeglass maker named Hans Lippershey invented the telescope in 1608. In 1609, Italian scientist Galileo Galilei was the first person to use a telescope to observe space. His telescope was so powerful that he discovered the four largest moons of Jupiter, the Moon's mountains, and the Sun's spots.

In 1668, English scientist Isaac Newton used a curved mirror to collect light through reflection. Mirrors are smooth surfaces that reflect most of the light that hits them. His simple improvement on telescope technology opened the way for larger, more exact telescopes to be built. Mirrors were much lighter than lenses. Much larger telescopes could now be built. Larger mirrors meant that telescopes could collect more light.

Top: *This refracting telescope belonged to Galileo Galilei. Bottom: In Isaac Newton's reflecting telescope, two metal mirrors inside reflect light. The primary, or main, mirror reflects light to a focus on the secondary mirror. The secondary mirror is set at an angle so that the light is reflected into the eyepiece lens for viewing.*

Computers and Telescopes

Between 1928 and 1948, the Hale Telescope was built on Mount Palomar in California. To create a mirror any larger than the Hale Telescope's 200-inch (5.1-m) mirror, scientists would need to make it thicker and house it in a much longer tube. Such a mirror would weigh more than 14 tons (12.7 t)! Bigger telescopes would have to wait for new technology.

Since the 1950s, computers and advances in **electronics** have helped to improve telescopes' vision without increasing their size. For example, computers can correct blurry starlight by keeping track of changes in the **atmosphere**. They send information on the changes to small mirrors that move to correct the blurriness and to sharpen the images. Computers also help telescope makers to shape the mirrors to have very exact curves. The idea is that no matter where light hits the **primary** mirror, it is reflected to a focus.

10

Top: *A Charge-Coupled Device is an electronic part that collects more light than does photographic film. A CCD makes a telescope more powerful so it will not need to be bigger.* Bottom: *The 36 small mirrors that make up the Keck I Telescope's primary mirror are moved by a computer twice per second. Together they act as one piece of glass.*

Charge-Coupled Device (CCD)

Photographic Plate

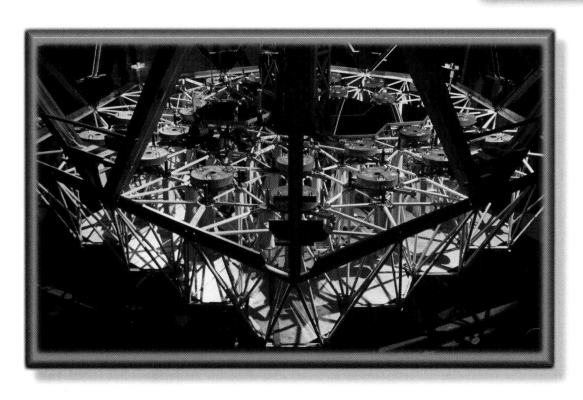

TECH KNOWLEDGE

Glass becomes molten at 2,100°F (1,148.9°C). It must cool slowly so that it does not crack. The Hale Telescope's first mirror cracked after one year of cooling, so a new mirror had to be made.

Making the Primary Mirror

The primary mirror is the most important part in a telescope. The primary mirror needs to be big enough to collect a lot of light. However, it cannot be so heavy that it sags or bends, or so thin that it changes shape in the wind. Primary mirrors are made of glass because glass is strong, low-priced, and able to be polished, or rubbed, to be very smooth. First the mirror is cast from molten glass, or glass that has been made liquid by heat. Once it cools, the flat glass, or blank, must be ground into a curved shape carefully to avoid making cracks. The glass must be polished so that it is exactly the right shape. It should be smoothed to within $\frac{1}{100}$ of the thickness of a human hair. The glass is then coated with a reflective metal, such as aluminum. The Hale Telescope's primary mirror took nearly 20 years to make.

The Hale Telescope's 200-inch (5.1-m) primary mirror is so exact that it can find the light from a candle that is 60,000 miles (96,560.6 km) away. The Hale Telescope has a secondary mirror that reflects the primary mirror's light into the eyepiece.

Mirror, Mirror

Today there are many methods for making large, exact primary mirrors. In the 1980s, Arizona's Steward Observatory Mirror Laboratory, or lab, created a process called spin-casting to reduce the time that was needed to grind a primary mirror. In this process, molten glass is quickly spun in an oven so that some of the glass moves toward the edges. When the glass cools, it is shaped like a bowl and does not need to be ground into a curved shape. The Mirror Lab spin-cast the mirrors for the Large **Binocular** Telescope that sits on Mount Graham in Arizona. One type of primary mirror, called a **segmented** mirror, uses smaller mirrors that fit together like floor tiles. For this mirror, astronomer Jerry Nelson suggested creating 36 six-sided mirrors. In another type, a honeycomb mirror, glass is cast in a pattern that looks like a bee's honeycomb. On top, there is a thin reflective surface.

14

The Keck telescopes in Mauna Kea, Hawaii, are two of the biggest telescopes in the world. Each of the 394-inch (10-m) primary mirrors in the Keck telescopes are actually made of 36 mirrors that are each 70 inches (177.8 cm) wide. Each was ground into a special shape. When the mirrors were linked, they formed a perfectly curved mirror.

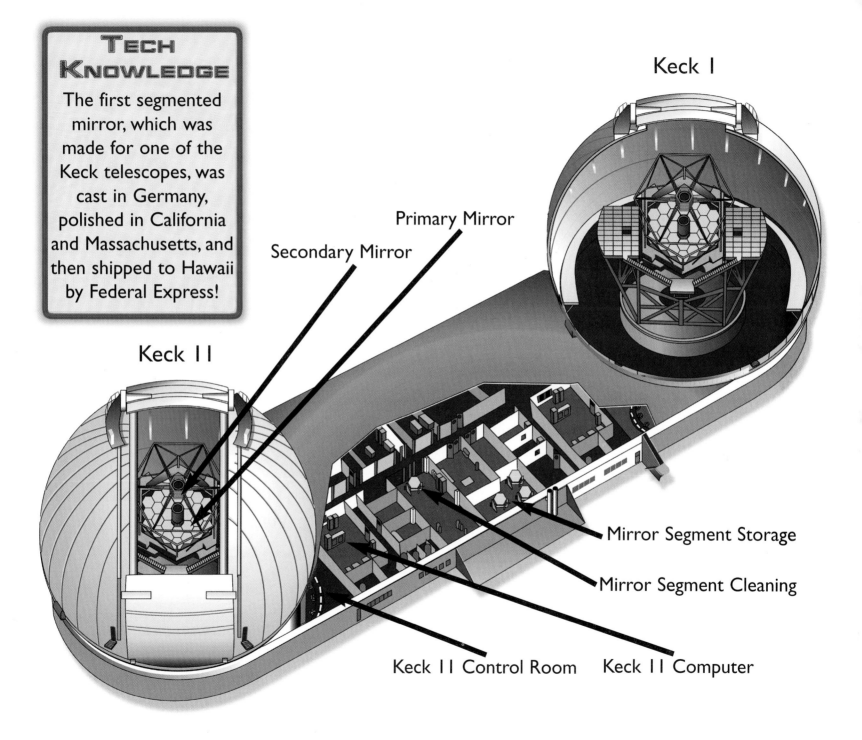

TECH KNOWLEDGE

The first segmented mirror, which was made for one of the Keck telescopes, was cast in Germany, polished in California and Massachusetts, and then shipped to Hawaii by Federal Express!

Keck I

Keck II

Secondary Mirror

Primary Mirror

Mirror Segment Storage

Mirror Segment Cleaning

Keck II Control Room

Keck II Computer

Radio Telescopes

Astronomers use radio telescopes to collect and measure radio waves from space. Radio waves can show us faraway objects that optical telescopes cannot, such as giant clouds of gas and very old stars that no longer give off light. Most radio telescopes, such as the Arecibo radio telescope in Puerto Rico, use a bowl-shaped reflector called a dish. Radio waves are longer than light waves. For this reason the dish of a radio telescope needs to be wider than the mirror of an optical telescope to focus the radio waves. Arecibo's dish is 1,000 feet (304.8 m) wide, the largest in the world. The bowl-shaped reflector focuses the waves onto an **antenna**. The antenna changes the waves into electric **signals**. A receiver strengthens and records these signals. Computers then change the signals into images.

The Arecibo radio telescope is built 167 feet (50.9 m) into the ground to protect it from Earth's humanmade radio waves. The dish's reflector is made of about 40,000 metal sheets of aluminum.

Observatories

Observatories are buildings that house telescopes. Optical telescope observatories are often built atop mountains far from cities, where there is excellent weather and dry air. The sky at these sites is mostly clear and free from air pollution and the bright lights of cities. An observatory is built with a dome, which has shutters that can close to protect the telescope from weather. An observatory is also designed to allow the telescope to move as it tracks objects in space. The dome and its shutters turn so that the telescope always has a clear view of the sky. The observatory's shape allows air to flow around the dome. This **aerodynamic** shape reduces air **turbulence**, which blurs the light. The dome shape for the 158-inch (4-m) Mayall Telescope in Arizona makes it the world's most aerodynamic observatory. Observatories also have many instruments that keep the air inside the dome cool.

18

Las Campanas Observatory is located high in the southern part of Chile's Atacama Desert. The 100-inch (2.5-m) Irénée du Pont telescope, which is seen here at night with its dome shutters open, has operated at the observatory since 1977.

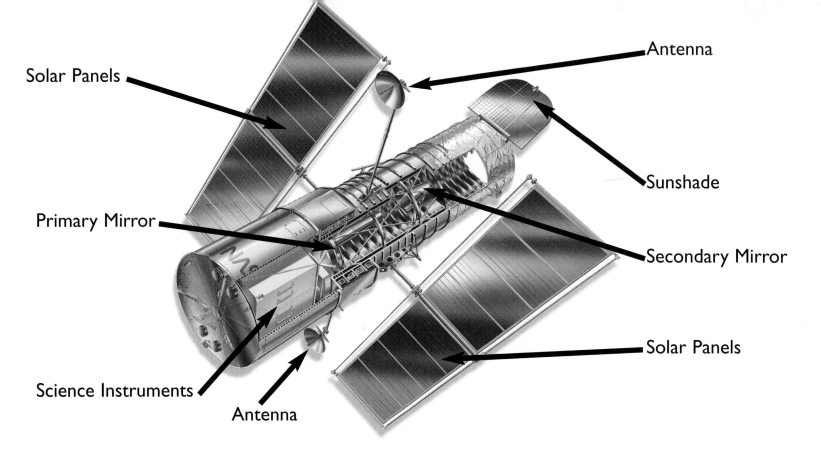

Solar Panels

Antenna

Primary Mirror

Sunshade

Secondary Mirror

Science Instruments

Solar Panels

Antenna

TIMELINE

1608 Dutch eyeglass lens maker Hans Lippershey invents the refraction telescope.

1609 Italian scientist Galileo Galilei improves Lippershey's telescope and begins to explore the heavens.

1668 English scientist Isaac Newton invents the reflection telescope.

1928–1948 The Hale Telescope at Mount Palomar, California, is built.

1963 The Arecibo radio telescope begins operations.

1990 The Hubble Space Telescope is sent into orbit.

1992 The Keck I Observatory is completed.

1996 The Keck II Observatory is completed.

2010 James Webb Space Telescope will be sent into space to help astronomers study the heavens.

The Hubble Space Telescope

    Although telescopes today are powerful, there are still limits to what scientists can see from Earth. In 1990, astronomers were ready to take the next step. That year, they sent the Hubble Space Telescope, an orbiting observatory, into space. It orbits 380 miles (611.6 km) above Earth. Because it orbits above Earth's atmosphere, the Hubble gives astronomers sharper images than do telescopes on Earth. The Hubble has a 94-inch (238.8-cm) primary mirror that collects light from the heavens. The secondary mirror reflects the light to smaller mirrors, which direct the light to scientific instruments. The instruments sense several kinds of radiation that humans cannot see. NASA astronomers use the information to make pictures of space. They have made many incredible discoveries, such as the Tadpole galaxy, because the Hubble can see light that is 12 billion years old.

The Hubble Space Telescope is 43 ½ feet (13.3 m) long and weighs 24,500 pounds (11,113 kg). Its solar panels are about 25 feet (7.6 m) long and weigh about 640 pounds (294.8 kg). The Hubble orbits Earth at a speed of 5 miles per second (8 km/s). It takes the Hubble 97 minutes to orbit Earth one time!

The Future of Telescope Technology

To help them study the farthest reaches of space, astronomers are creating new huge telescopes called megatelescopes. They will need to make even bigger telescopes than Keck I and Keck II, perhaps having mirrors half the size of a U.S. football field!

Scientists are now working on the Hubble's replacement, the James Webb Space Telescope. The Webb telescope, to be completed in 2010, will be able to see farther into space than the Hubble can because its primary mirror will be able to collect more light. The mirror will be at least 20 feet (6 m) wide, more than two and one-half times wider than Hubble's primary mirror. Astronomers hope to use this new technology to find planets that have oceans and atmospheres like our own, planets that could possibly support life!

Glossary

aerodynamic (ar-oh-dy-NA-mik) Designed to move through the air easily.

antenna (an-TEH-nah) A metal object used to send and receive signals.

astronomers (uh-STRAH-nuh-merz) People who study the Sun, Moon, planets, and stars.

atmosphere (AT-muh-sfeer) The layer of gases around an object in space. On Earth, this layer is air.

binocular (bih-NAH-kyuh-lur) Using two telescopes in one mount to give more power than just one.

electronics (ih-lek-TRAH-niks) The science that deals with electricity and how it works.

focus (FOH-kis) To make clear; a point at which rays of light meet after being refracted by a lens or reflected by a mirror, or the process of bringing light to that point with a lens or mirror.

galaxies (GA-lik-seez) Large groups of stars and the planets that circle them.

NASA (NA-suh) National Aeronautics and Space Administration; the U.S. space agency.

optical (OP-tih-kul) Having to do with the sense of sight; designed to help one see.

primary (PRY-mer-ee) Main; greatest in importance.

radiation (ray-dee-AY-shun) Rays of light, heat, or energy that spread outward from something.

radio (RAY-dee-oh) A type of wave that comes from objects, such as hot gases, in space.

reflect (rih-FLEKT) To throw back light, heat, or sound.

segmented (SEG-men-ted) Having many smaller pieces.

signals (SIG-nulz) Currents, messages, sounds, or other signs that are sent.

technology (tek-NAH-luh-jee) The way that a people do something using tools, and the tools that they use.

turbulence (TER-byuh-lens) The state of being stirred up.

X rays (EKS RAYZ) Rays that can pass through matter that light rays cannot.

Index

Web Sites

Due to the changing nature of Internet links, PowerKids Press has developed an online list of Web sites related to the subject of this book. This site is updated regularly. Please use this link to access the list:

www.powerkidslinks.com/kgit/telescop/